ENOUGH

An Answer in a World Full of Wants

Peter Mike Hoffman

ISBN 978-1-64003-639-0 (Paperback)
ISBN 978-1-64003-640-6 (Digital)

Covenant Books, Inc.
11661 Hwy 707
Murrells Inlet, SC 29576
www.covenantbooks.com

CONTENTS

ACKNOWLEDGEMENTS

To those whom I love endlessly such as my parents, whose sacrifice and support, remain my strength and determination today. My wife Amy who has taught me how to allow laughter and being real to be lived out together. The entire Hoffman Family whose presence and affection is always worth the four-hour drive for the three-hour visit! Lastly to the countless others who have impacted me more than I have impacted them. Beginning with John Gordy, Bill Bjork, The Davis family, Donnie Ream, Carlyle Naylor and many others who have allowed me to witness God proving he is enough.

FOREWORD

I first met Mike Hoffman at Naval Support Activity (NSA) in Naples, Italy, in 2001. Mike was a Dental Technician and I was one of the NSA Chaplains. He became acquainted with the Chapel community shortly after his arrival and began attending the Full Gospel Fellowship worship services. It wasn't long before Mike began to stand out in the Chapel community; not because he sought to be in the limelight, but because of his faithfulness to God, the community of faith, and the Italian and American civilian personnel.

While most military personnel are committed to their work, I was struck by this young Sailor's selflessness, perseverance, and compassion. Mike felt a strong sense of calling to serve, which he expressed each week. He arrived early to services to make himself available to help the Chapel staff. When our congregation outgrew the Chapel, we moved our Sunday services to the Base Theater, which required early morning set-up and late morning breakdown. Mike was always there to help. When we initiated a Singles' Group, he was present, providing leadership to ensure the group became a vital part of the Chapel ministry, successful and sustainable.

I was impressed when Mike began writing devotions for our congregation and base personnel. Each morning as we arrived at work, his devotional was waiting for us in our email inboxes. He was intent on helping us to begin our workdays in the right frame of mind.

I thought this would last for a short season. Anyone who has written regularly is aware of the discipline and energy this requires. No one would have faulted him if he decided to either write less frequently or stop altogether. He did stop. Five years later!

If that wasn't enough in and of itself, Mike also completed his Associates degree during his off-duty hours. All the while, he kept his Chapel commitments and performed in outstanding fashion in the Dental Department. It became rather clear that Mike was being called into ministry.

When I asked him to preach, he was eager to learn and worked painstakingly to put together a sermon that would honor God and encourage his brothers and sisters in Christ. We went through the process together, step-by-step. He was teachable and adapted quickly. Mike preached well.

In time, Mike was reassigned to Pensacola, Florida, for his final assignment prior to being honorably discharged. He moved back to Arizona, started working for the U.S. Postal Service, and quickly advanced. He married a beautiful woman, Amy, and furthered his studies by earning a Master of Ministry from Phoenix Seminary. During the course of this time, he became aware of an elderly community without a pastor. Without hesitation, he volunteered to serve as their pastor and began caring for many who no longer had family or friends to visit them. Mike brought dignity and meaning to their lives through genuine care and compassion, and he continues to do so to this day.

What Mike shares in this book emerges from a life well acquainted with hardships and challenges, failures and successes. And you will soon realize that it is "Enough" to carry you through your own difficulties and trials. Why? Because he writes of the Person who is always enough…Jesus Christ.

Thank you again, Mike! You continue to be an inspiration to this ol' salty Sailor.

Peace and grace,
John C. Gordy
Lieutenant Commander
Chaplain Corps
U.S. Navy (Ret)

ENDORSEMENTS

"Culture has hijacked the soul's desire for the infinite, so that we are left feeling empty, a very difficult, lonely place. Mike Hoffman points the reader to God, the only source of eternal contentment. Enough is life-giving."

John DelHousaye
Associate Professor of New Testament and
Spiritual Formation, Phoenix Seminary

"Making sense of the stories of our life can be difficult and disorienting. Mr. Hoffman takes stories of his life and his love for Scripture and combines them into new stories of application and inspiration that make sense. Enough reflects Mr. Hoffman's heart as a servant of Jesus and of humankind. He is vulnerable, while not being accusatory or succumbing to victim-mentality."

Dr. Carlyle Naylor
Emotional intelligence life coach,
bible-based pastor for 25 years and author
of Emotalerting, The Art of Managing the

Moment—a number one best seller that helps people understand and manage their emotions.

My friend and former student Mike Hoffman is on to something with this book, and that's the emptiness of people as compared to the sufficiency of God. As Mike demonstrates, the heart of men constantly seeks more in every possible area of need or activity; the grace of God alone supplies us with enough. "The Lord is my Shepherd; I am never in need" (King David, Psalm 23:1). Let Mike explain in this helpful little book how David's experience with God can be yours as well. "May the Lord of peace give you peace at all times and in every way" (2 Thess. 3:16).

Dr. Bill Bjork
Senior Pastor
Grace Bible Church
Sun City, Arizona
Adjunct Faculty, Phoenix Seminary,
Scottsdale, Arizona

INTRODUCTION

An Answer in a World Full of Wants

Pornography, sex trafficking, infidelity, substance abuse, hoarding, overspending, bullying others (particularly on social media), and judging one another... This egocentric world we find ourselves living in is full of wants and a never-ending desire of satisfying self. The more we obtain, the more we crave. Our culture and even some within Christendom are finding themselves malnourished. No, not in the sense of their hunger not being met but that they are still found truly not happy with the life they have chosen. Experiencing an abundant life is not happening because they have failed to experience that which is enough.

As I reflect back on my life and through the pages of history as recorded in the Bible, I discover some things not only about myself but about others. Five years in the US Navy, thirteen years serving the public working for the United States Postal Service, and eleven years as a bivocational pastor have led me to visualize a constant theme that is ever present. This theme is found all throughout humanity and is best described as not having enough. The struggles I have faced and find myself facing today is whether or not I believe I have been given access to having enough. My desire for more and more or to be liked on social media all stems from a misunderstanding of a simple word.

The word, indeed, is *enough*, and most likely, as you ponder the word, you are thinking one or two things. The first is you find yourself saying, "Enough, I never have enough." The second, which you are saying even louder, is "Enough is enough." Yes, you have had it up to here, most likely the length of your height, and you are longing for a solution. You are looking for a remedy to cure your lack of not having enough, all the while hoping to satisfy your desire of always wanting more. Regardless of how you find yourself using the word, venturing through this book will help you, as I have discovered, find the answer.

Every week, as I show up to serve at a retirement community, I am reminded that life is both short and precious. In the three years I have been their volunteer pastor, I have met both those whose lives are a bubbling brook and those who are dried-out cistern. You can either live your life in want and be angry that you don't have enough (dried cistern) or live as you have been designed (bubbling brook). Yes, how you and I were designed was not with lacking anything but with having enough.

> And God blessed them, and God said unto them, Be fruitful, and multiply, and replenish the earth, and subdue it: and have dominion over the fish of the sea, and over the fowl of the air, and over every living thing that moveth upon the earth. (Genesis 1:28 KJV)

As I interact with those in their eighties and nineties, I can tell you firsthand that how you discover having enough only comes through experiencing the One who is. Why, because neither age nor wealth acquired will fix one's desire of having enough.

Just ask the lady who simply came to the service to observe and ensure I actually moved the chair's back for bingo. Or the gal who made a single appearance to tell me I needed to switch the service time even though everyone else was agreeing with the time. I'm by no means picking on these ladies because as you read through each chapter you will discover the times when I certainly embraced the same attitude. Yes, having this mind-set and acting as if you don't have enough robbed me and will rob you from experiencing true satisfaction. We will never be satisfied until we fully grasp that which we have been given is all we need. Whether it is in the area of wanting (never satisfied), winning (at all costs), working (for who you love), winking (staying committed), wronging (extending grace), wasting (over-indulging), or welcoming (getting beyond self), each of these seven chapters show us how we actually do have enough. At the end of each chapter, you will find a section called "Experiencing Enough," which is how practically individuals put into use what you just discovered within that specific chapter. Also included at the onset and end of each chapter our quotes, whether they are songs or scriptures, to help capture the fundamentals that form each chapter.

Lastly, in all honesty, this journey might be difficult for you because discovering how one finds enough requires one to rethink what our current culture proclaims to us each day. Even though the pain is like getting pierced by a needle and an IV inserted, the end result is you receiving the much-needed vaccine. Whether it's trying to satisfy your soul with wants or winning at all cost, understanding the true meaning of enough is crucial for our personal and spiritual success. Each chapter is designed with the purpose of discovering that which enough is. I am not a self-proclaimed expert, but through different experiences in my own life and through the lives of prominent biblical figures, I hope, as I have, you will find true fulfillment.

And God is able to bless you abundantly, so that in all things at all times, having all that you need, you will abound in every good work. (2 Corinthians 9:8 NIV)

The question then is how? How do you discover in this world full of wants that you have all you need? Take this journey with me, and you will not only uncover how but also discover the validity of these words proclaimed so long ago.

Taste and see that the LORD is good; blessed is the one who takes refuge in him. Fear the LORD, you his holy people, for those who fear him lack nothing. The lions may grow weak and hungry, but those who seek the LORD *lack no good thing*. Come, my children, listen to me; I will teach you the fear of the LORD. (Psalm 34:8–11)

CHAPTER 1

Wanting: What Do You Want

I've gotta have more and
more, what I got
That's what they make
money for, what I got
I sold my soul like a whore, what
I got I will never be satisfied
I will never be satisfied
I will never be satisfied
until it ends in tears.
Corey Glover and Vernon
Reid, "Never Satisfied"

Wow, those are some lyrics, but how fitting as we began this journey in discussing the ever-growing need of wanting more. The truth is, we all want a multitude of things. I call them things because usually that is all they end up being. Yes, things that have taken up space in the garage or the attic or the spare bedroom that you had high hopes for when you purchased them. The common expression today is "coming out of the closet." The lyrics above simply open the door to the reality of what we actually tell ourselves. My actual closet and yours is proof that we are wedged into believing that we need more. All the clothes, hobbies, and a hodgepodge of our things are actually keeping us hidden in the closet and not dealing with this tragic truth. We all long for and share a common desire which says, we need more. No matter what we acquire, we still find ourselves unsatisfied.

For me, it started with the age-old question "What do you want to do when you grow up?" Do you remember that question? Don't feel bad if those days have slipped your mind, but maybe you do recall the question proposed in your high school yearbook. You know that picture of you standing there with the caption that read, "Most likely to be." My guess is that you or none of your friends responded with this statement, "I do not want to be anything but simply want to have enough." The reason for this is because that would not be dreaming big enough. By not supersizing your desire, you can already hear others, including family members, say, "Why are you selling yourself short?" For me, my big dream was extra large. What I wanted to do when I grew up was to be a dentist. How about you? What is or was your big dream? Have you achieved it, and if you have, how is that working out for you? In all honesty has accomplishing your childhood dream proven to be enough, satisfying your desire of wanting more?

There is nothing wrong with fulfilling a childhood dream, but what I discovered in the process of trying to fulfill such a dream changed my entire perspective. I remember asking myself while studying in college, how is becoming a dentist going to honor God? This question, for some reason, became clear a few years later as I was serving in the United States Navy. Before we get any further, a bigger question has emerged, which is what you are probably asking yourself: "Why God?" Well, because God has revealed himself to me in unique and unfathomable ways. The personal stories shared within this book are just a few moments of where God has drawn me near to him, solidifying for me the need to bring God up in our conversation. Yes, just as I would those whom I respect in my life, such as my wife, family, and or friends. Now back to the end of my freshman year of college.

You see, after one year at the University of Arizona, the challenges of school and the need to pay tuition for college led me to join the Navy. I joined the Navy with the intent of living out my childhood dream and in the process allow Uncle Sam to pay the bill. However, as time went on, I was able to answer the question that had been lodged in my mind. My conclusion, I could not honor God by becoming a dentist. Now this answer was only for me. I knew it was only for me because when I tried to justify my desire for becoming a dentist it became even clearer why I shouldn't. I discovered I shouldn't become a dentist because of my reasoning for me being a dentist in the first place. My deep-down desire for becoming a dentist was to fulfill my longing of having enough. Yes, enough money, enough clout, and enough of everything else to go around.

What I haven't told you is that in the few years leading up to being able to answer my internal question, I began reading through stories of those longing to be satisfied. One particular story is given by a powerful man named King Solomon. His position, power, and wealth afforded him the ability to do what he wanted to do. His mission was simple—discover the threshold of acquiring enough, just as I was doing in my quest in becoming a doctor of dentistry. As I read through King Solomon's conquests, I actually was jealous until I read his conclusion.

> The end of the matter; all has been heard.
> Fear God and keep his commandments,
> for this is the whole duty of man. For God
> will bring every deed into judgment, with
> every secret thing, whether good or evil.
> (Ecclesiastes 12:13–14 ESV)

His conclusion made more sense as I reflected on what God was doing in me. Through this reflective process, I discovered I was wrestling with what I wanted, regardless of what God wanted for me. This perspective shift is what allowed me to ask, "How is being a dentist going to help me honor God?" I would have never asked this question if I didn't discover what I was actually longing for, and that was to simply have enough. Why, because in reality I was confused between what I wanted and that which enough is. The longing for more always covers up seeing what God actually desires for us to embrace. This is where we find ourselves being disoriented. We think, "I will have enough when I fulfill all my wants." Whether it's picking a career field or buying the next generation of a cell phone, we remain desiring more, because we are trying to make enough happen. To avoid confusion, we can never make enough happen, because enough has already happened. Yes, enough is not found in an occupation or an education but rather in the one who formed our minds in the first place.

Case in point, King Nebuchadnezzar longed to fulfill what he wanted only to discover that what he longed for only led to confusion and an episode of losing his mind, as recorded in Daniel 4:28–33. However, like the prodigal son, who (which we will explore later) came to his senses, we find Nebuchadnezzar embracing the same mind-set as seen with King Solomon.

At the end of the days I, Nebuchadnezzar, lifted my eyes to heaven, and my reason returned to me, and I blessed the Most High, and praised and honored him who lives forever, for his dominion is an everlasting dominion, and his kingdom endures from generation to generation; all the inhabitants of the earth are accounted as nothing, and he does according to his will among the host of heaven and among the inhabitants of the earth; and none can stay his hand or say to him, "What have you done?" At the same time my reason returned to me, and for the glory of my kingdom, my majesty and splendor returned to me. My counselors and my lords sought me, and I was established in my kingdom, and still more greatness was added to me. Now I, Nebuchadnezzar, praise and extol and honor the King of heaven, for all his works are right and his ways are just; and those who walk in pride he is able to humble. (Daniel 4:34–37 ESV)

This, indeed, is the starting point in discovering that which is enough. The longing for wanting more is a fear that we won't have enough. The question is who or what are you lifting your eyes toward? For me, I discovered my eyes needed to be looking at God, the same God who both King Solomon and King Nebuchadnezzar fixed their eyes on. They zoomed in on God because God showed them how to handle their longing for wanting more.

How we overcome our longing for wanting more is by trusting in the one who has a continual supply. Yes, sometimes that continual supply is shared in unexpected ways.

> Then the word of the Lord came to him, "Arise, go to Zarephath, which belongs to Sidon, and dwell there. Behold, I have commanded a widow there to feed you." So he arose and went to Zarephath. And when he came to the gate of the city, behold, a widow was there gathering sticks. And he called to her and said, "Bring me a little water in a vessel, that I may drink." And as she was going to bring it, he called to her and said, "Bring me a morsel of bread in your hand." And she said, "As the Lord your God lives, I have nothing baked, only a handful of flour in a jar and a little oil in a jug. And now I am gathering a couple of sticks that I may go in and prepare it for myself and my son, that we may eat it and die." And Elijah said to her, "Do not fear; go and

do as you have said. But first make me a little cake of it and bring it to me, and afterward make something for yourself and your son. For thus says the Lord, the God of Israel, 'The jar of flour shall not be spent, and the jug of oil shall not be empty, until the day that the Lord sends rain upon the earth.'" And she went and did as Elijah said. And she and he and her household ate for many days. The jar of flour was not spent, neither did the jug of oil become empty, according to the word of the Lord that he spoke by Elijah. (1 Kings 17:8–16 ESV)

God told Elijah he was going to feed him so he needed to trust and go where God was sending him. When he got to the widow, she had to trust in what Elijah was asking her to do even though it didn't make sense. By them trusting in God, who was wanting to supply their need, their fear of not having enough was removed.

I remember when God provided for my family in an unexpected way. About eight months before I received orders to my duty assignment in Naples, Italy, I bought my first brand-new car. This car was going be driven to Wichita Falls, Texas, where I was heading for what in the Navy is called C school. This school was six months and was going to train me in how to fabricate dental prosthetics. By now, in my short Navy experience, I had enough rank to be able to live off base, which meant I needed a car. On leave before heading to Texas, I purchased a four-door silver 2000 Plymouth Neon with a standard transmission. I made it to Texas and used that car often. I did live off base and drove to and from school along with taking a few trips to Dallas and to San Antonio to watch the Arizona Wildcats play in the NCAA Basketball Tournament.

As my time in Texas drew to an end, I had to decide what I was going to do with my car. The simple answer was to have the Navy ship the car overseas to Naples, Italy, which is where I would spend the next two years. No big deal. They ship the car; I fly home to Phoenix for leave, then fly back to Texas so the Navy could send me on my way to Naples. For some reason, I started asking around about sending a new car overseas. I reached out to those who had once served in Naples and to my sponsor who was currently serving in Naples. I received mixed answers on whether it was a good idea. When the time came to make the final decision, I had a strong feeling—like I did when I finally asked myself if I should become a dentist—that I needed to leave my car at my parents' house in Phoenix. My mom doesn't drive, so my parents have only had one car and had no need for another vehicle—so I thought. My car was just going to stay in the carport, and my dad would drive it a few times just to keep the car in running order.

Fast forward to about ten months left in my stay in Naples, and my parents fell on some hard times because work in construction for my dad became slow. They couldn't make the payment on their vehicle, so it ended up being repossessed about two months prior to my leaving Naples. This was devastating to them, and I couldn't help them financially because I had my own financial obligations. However, they had what they needed in their driveway, and of course, I gave them the approval of driving my car solely.

This, indeed, helped them out tremendously, and for the next few years, this enabled them to get back on their feet financially. Why a few years? Because this is, as I look back, where God actually came through abundantly. God took, like the widow, my little car that I trusted to Him and kept supplying my parents with transportation. Yes, all because I listened to the longing of not sending the car overseas. By not sending the car to Naples, my car wasn't going to be sent directly to my next duty station, which was Pensacola, Florida. My parents would have never had access to the car if I listened to my own needs instead of listening to God's prompting. The amazing thing is that as I spent two years in Naples and one year in Pensacola, on countless times others provided for me by giving me rides. I indeed thanked them for their kindness and generosity, but little did they know that God, through one simple ride, was actually meeting two needs! How we find ourselves not wanting is through trusting God. We stop ourselves from wanting by looking to Him. All the remaining chapters provide the evidence for your heart to direct your eyes to be looking not at *what* but *whom*.

> Lord is my Shepherd, I shall not want
> Takes away my fears, you restore my soul
> Off into the sky, the dead in Christ arise
> To be with you forever, see with the clear-
> est eyes
> Quench my inner thirst, there's some-
> thing more in life
> No money, cars, relationships compare to
> joy in Christ
> Love that falls from selfish ones that like
> to flirt with self-destruct
> No need to strut, know what I want, to
> keep it, but my God's enough.
> Marcus Gray et al., "God Is Enough"

Experiencing Enough

- You will never know what God desires you to have until you ask Him.
- You will never ask Him if you don't include Him in what you long for.

- The reason for including Him is to determine if what you want is simply to have what you want or what he desires for you to have.
- By only desiring the things you want, you find yourself needing more and more, which keeps you bound to the mind-set of never having enough.
- Because of who God is, he will always be enough, which is why your eyes need to remain fixed on Him.

CHAPTER 2

Winning: The Game Show of Life

We are the champions, my friends,
And we'll keep on fighting 'til the end.
We are the champions.
We are the champions.
No time for losers
'Cause we are the champions,
of the world.
Freddie Mercury, "We are
the Champions"

For me, winning wasn't everything, but loosing was never an option. At least this is what I told myself. Whether it was sports or planning a vacation, my competitive side took over. Yes, the side that says, "At all costs, I will do what it takes." Here recently, my wife and I with her siblings auditioned for the game show *Family Feud*. Of course, we were convinced we did enough to be one of the families to get a postcard in the mail informing us we were selected. In fact, we were told at the second and final audition of the day by one of the producers that we were "the most unique family she had seen all day." To our shock, of course, the weeks went by, and we received no postcard. During the short time after the audition, I even thought maybe there was a problem with our mail being delivered incorrectly. I discovered this wasn't the case but that we were just not selected. This time, however, I didn't find myself getting angry but recalling these words.

> For everyone who exalts himself will be humbled, and he who humbles himself will be exalted. (Luke 14:11 ESV)

In chapter 1, I made mention to the process of a few years, actually about four years, which opened my eyes to viewing life through a different lens. In the first year of the four-year process, I had an eye-opening experience regarding winning. As I said, I am very competitive so much so that I would get angry with my performance, or lack thereof, during any competition. In my first year of being in the Navy, I was stationed on an island in the middle of the Indian Ocean called Diego Garcia. This was an isolated duty assignment in which no families were allowed, and the tour lasted one year.

Of course, to keep the service members active, intramural sports and tournaments were always going on. From softball to volleyball, running 5Ks to darts, just about every sport. Even drinking was a competition. When I arrived on the island, I was told the infamous saying, "You will either leave here a hunk, drunk, or chunk." During a particular basketball game, I happened to find myself, all by myself, at the end of the court. The rest of the team was at the other end, and the previous play didn't go my way. In a still, small voice, I remember hearing, "Why are you so angered?" To me, everything stopped, and I felt as if I needed to deal with this question. That day, something in me changed, and I was humbled in the area of needing to win. My desire changed, and I begin seeing any and every competition as just that, a competition. After this experience, I found myself enjoying playing instead of using the sport to fulfill my desire of winning. Because of this experience, when I finally read through the book of Genesis and came across the story of Joseph, I could comprehend why Joseph could respond the way he did to his brothers. The story of Joseph is found in Genesis chapter 37 through chapter 50, which I encourage you to read to uncover every detail.

Joseph, instead of being killed, was sold into slavery by his brothers, who were angered at him because of his boastful attitude. Joseph along the way experienced a list of trials, such as being wrongly accused of rape and forgotten about for two years. While in prison, Joseph maintained a humbled attitude, earning favor with the jailor. Joseph was eventually released from prison and got the position of being second-in-command to Pharaoh. Joseph interpreted a dream, which he acted upon by storing up grain in the abundant years because a famine was on the horizon. The famine hit, and those outside of Egypt were in desperate need. Joseph's brothers ended up traveling to Egypt for food. To their shock, Joseph, their long-lost brother, now had the power to either display humility or win the day by getting revenge. I believe Joseph didn't choose to win the fight against his brothers, seeking revenge because of the many years Joseph was humbled. He endured his own struggles. Yes, like what I experienced, Joseph embraced the idea that winning isn't everything. We find this to be true by how Joseph responded to his brothers when he was reunited with them.

> Then Joseph could not control himself before all those who stood by him. He cried, "Make everyone go out from me." So no one stayed with him when Joseph made himself known to his brothers. And he wept aloud, so that the Egyptians heard it, and the household of Pharaoh heard it. And Joseph said to his brothers, "I am Joseph! Is my father still alive?" But his brothers could not answer him,

for they were dismayed at his presence. So Joseph said to his brothers, "Come near to me, please." And they came near. And he said, "I am your brother, Joseph, whom you sold into Egypt. And now do not be distressed or angry with yourselves because you sold me here, for God sent me before you to preserve life. For the famine has been in the land these two years, and there are yet five years in which there will be neither plowing nor harvest. And God sent me before you to preserve for you a remnant on earth, and to keep alive for you many survivors. So it was not you who sent me here, but God. He has made me a father to Pharaoh, and lord of all his house and ruler over all the land of Egypt. Hurry and go up to my father and say to him, 'Thus says your son Joseph, God has made me lord of all Egypt. Come down to me; do not tarry. You shall dwell in the land of Goshen, and you shall be near me, you and your children and your children's children, and your flocks, your herds, and all that you have. There I will provide for you, for there are yet five years of famine to come, so that you and your household, and all that you have, do not come to poverty.'" (Genesis 45:1–11 ESV)

I truly relate to verse 5 and how Joseph told his brothers not to be "angry with yourselves." Today, as we look at my life and those like Joseph, we discover that how we win in this life is through humility. Yes, from experiencing this firsthand, I was able to write the poem below when I graduated seminary. The reason I was able to write such a poem is because of being humbled that day on the basketball court. Before I leave you with the poem, I propose a question and some final thoughts. Does your desire to win overrule the humility you display toward others?

When winning is your top priority, you actually lose in the game show called life. I understand this now because of seeing those times in life when humility ruled the day—for example, when I drove over the corner of a customer's wall. I didn't see that the wall protruded out away from their built-in mailbox. As I drove away, after putting mail in their box, I broke out several blocks from driving over the wall. I knew this would get me fired because I was still on the ninety-day probationary period. Even though I drove down to the end of the neighborhood, saying to myself I couldn't risk telling the customer, I had to go back. As I went up to the house, I noticed that the wall up toward the house was also busted out, and to my surprise, there were workers in the backyard using a tractor. The house, as I discovered, was being remodeled, but I humbled myself and informed the workers anyway of what I did. To my shock, they said no problem. They actually informed me that they were the ones who drove over the wall up by the house earlier that day with the tractor. They ensured me it wasn't a problem since that entire wall was going to be taken out. They thanked me for my honesty, and everyone went back to work as normal. No complaints to my boss, no loss of job, and a win for my conscience, allowing me to sleep that night.

Winning from God's perspective, which is the message behind the story of Joseph and these two stories from my personal life, is satisfying because they help us see how God fulfills our longing to be first.

> Give, and it will be given to you. A good measure, pressed down, shaken together and running over, will be poured into your lap. For with the measure you use, it will be measured to you. (Luke 6:38 NIV)

Longing to be first overrides our desire to serve others, which keeps us longing for more self-serving victories. However, on the flip side, humility is what stirs in us the need to help others, which satisfies our soul, pointing us to the fact that we have enough. Discovering this is how I was able to pen this poem.

What If...

What if you were born at just the right moment, displaying your birth to the world that humanity begins and ends with life?

What if your childhood was proof that laughter and tears are the building blocks that advanced both you and your parents?

What if your parents' financial struggle, stresses, deceases, and pain were your hands-on experience in answering life's greatest question, which is God always provides?

What if the decades your parents remain married showed you more than an oath but His lasting love?

What if being the minority at your high school is your clarity of what the kingdom of God is truly like?

What if the university you attended became the reason you are able now to bear down through life's worst trials?

What if the lives of the loved ones who have passed on remain your hypothesis that renders the one and only solution, the cross?

What if your enlistment propelled you to think beyond your duty and receive your greatest reward, which is to serve others?

What if your occupation of carrying mail stamped into your soul the daily reminder of Him delivering you?

What if you arrived to celebrate graduating seminary but left with the realization that He intended you to be there all along, not so you could question what if but that He is!

Experiencing Enough

- Winning should never override humility.
- Humility is how everyone wins because others like Joseph's brothers would never experience the abundance of God's provision if humility wasn't shown.

- As those who witness God's overflowing mercy, the correct response is to give thanks rather than ask for more.
- If you are unable to give thanks as you compete in the game called life, your desire to win is whom you are serving.
- Serving self never is filling but always leaves you thinking you don't have enough.
- By embracing humility through any and every competition, you will always be satisfied.

CHAPTER 3

Working: For Whom You Love

You load sixteen tons, what do you get?
Another day older and deeper in debt
Saint Peter don't you call
me 'cause I can't go
I owe my soul to the company store.
Merle Travis, "Sixteen Tons"

All of us have a reason why we work, and all of us work for someone, even if that someone is you. I made mention earlier that the reason for joining the Navy was to serve my own desires. However, because of an experience at boot camp, my attitude changed, and I learned that while I was working for my country, I was going to serve others. Boot camp was an eight-week adventure that required a lot of patience and surrendering self. About four weeks in, I discovered on my Sunday free time, I was not getting paid. At the time, 160 hours of pay missing from my paycheck was a huge deal. This meant all the yelling and screaming and waking up before the sunrise to exercise was for my own pleasure and at my own expense. My conclusion was logical: tell my recruit division commander, the Navy's version of a drill instructor, and he will help me get paid for working. Obviously, this is what I was doing, working for the Navy, and because I was working, never mind the miserable conditions, I deserved to get paid. Unfortunately, my wonderful RDC couldn't fix my pay problem because his job was to monitor recruits like me and not pay them. For some reason, he wanted to be nice, maybe because it was Sunday. He told me that sometime during the upcoming week he would send me to the personnel office to fix the problem.

This sounded easy, but there was a dilemma with going to the personnel office, and that is you had to walk across the base by yourself and experience a possible crossfire. Not a literal crossfire but an occasional ambush by some other RDC who just wanted to cause a recruit some grief. Yes, RDCs who would be marching their whole division would halt their division if they saw a recruit walking by themselves just to allow their division to see another recruit being integrated. The RDC would see the recruit and would say, "Recruit, halt!" and then walk over to confront the recruit face-to-face, asking them the dreaded question, "Where are you going, Recruit?" After the recruit who is in shock answers the question, the

RDC then would say, "Do you have your chit?" which was basically what you would have—like in school, a hall pass—so you could travel to where the chit was saying you were going. A recruit caught without a chit was in big trouble. Lucky for me, I did have a chit, and I did make it to the personnel office without being stopped. However, what happened next was just as bad as being stopped.

As I approached the personnel desk, there happen to be a lady in civilian clothes working behind the desk. I informed the lady that I was there because I was not getting paid. As she looked over at another desk to a coworker who was wearing a Navy uniform, she said to me, "Before we get your pay straightened out, we have a few things for you to do, like dump the trash bins." My heart immediately started pounding, and I was furious inside. I wanted to definitely cuss this lady out and at the same time, I felt like the wind had been taken out of my sails. I wanted to tell her, "How dare you!" and then give her a piece of my mind. However, for some reason, I couldn't. As I still think about this story today, I remember the peace that came over me. I was indeed angered but listened and did what she said. I guess I earned my keep, because she did fix my pay problem.

So there I go, heading back to a possible crossfire, this time with a whole new attitude. A gracious attitude about what it means to serve others as Christ served each of us on the cross. As I walked back to the barracks, I vividly recall making this connection. Yes, on how Christ served me and allowed me to do the same toward this lady without complaining or cussing her out. I remember specifically thanking Jesus for allowing me to keep my mouth shut and render service unto a lady who actually was not my boss at all. That day, God changed my perspective from only thinking about working and getting paid to honoring him through serving others in the process. As I look back on my five years of naval service, I can honestly say, after receiving three Navy and Marine Corps achievement medals, countless letters of commendation and letters of appreciation, that I proudly served my country and the U.S. Navy. I left you in suspense in chapter 1 regarding the purpose behind departing the Navy. In 2004 when I no longer was known as government property, I became an ordinary civilian. With my DD214 in hand and GI Bill, I left the Navy with the intent of pursuing a college education. By this time, I had already earned an associates of arts degree. My purpose for going to school was to earn a bachelor's degree then move onto seminary to enter into full-time ministry.

There was one problem, which is why most all of us have to work. I needed to provide for myself while going to school. As a veteran, I was allowed to take the postal service exam to become a letter carrier. The day I signed up to take the exam, through the input of family and friends who were city carriers, I also filled out an application to become a temporary employee of the postal service. Well, to my surprise, I was hired right away as a casual carrier (temporary employee). Fast forward almost thirteen years, and I remain employed with the United States Postal Service and currently work as a full-time city carrier in Phoenix. I did finish my bachelor's and seminary degree within this thirteen-year time frame and am currently waiting to enter into full-time ministry. It's in this process of waiting that I have been reminded of someone who also waited while they worked.

> Jacob loved Rachel. And he said, "I will serve you seven years for your younger daughter Rachel." Laban said, "It is better that I give her to you than that I should give her to any other man; stay with me." So Jacob served seven years for Rachel, and they seemed to him but a few days because of the love he had for her. Then Jacob said to Laban, "Give me my wife that I may go in to her, for my time is completed." So Laban gathered together all the people of the place and made a feast. But in the evening he took his daughter Leah and brought her to Jacob, and he went in to her. (Laban gave his female servant Zilpah to his daughter Leah to be her servant.)

45

And in the morning, behold, it was Leah! And Jacob said to Laban, "What is this you have done to me? Did I not serve with you for Rachel? Why then have you deceived me?" Laban said, "It is not so done in our country, to give the younger before the firstborn. Complete the week of this one, and we will give you the other also in return for serving me another seven years." Jacob did so, and completed her week. Then Laban gave him his daughter Rachel to be his wife. (Laban gave his female servant Bilhah to his daughter Rachel to be her servant.) So Jacob went in to Rachel also, and he loved Rachel more than Leah, and served Laban for another seven years. (Genesis 29:18–30 ESV)

What I gather from this story is that Jacob's love for Rachel didn't waver, and for fourteen years, he worked for whom he loved. This resonates with me because this is what I have been doing for the last thirteen years—I have been working for whom I love. No, not the postal service but for the one who had been calling me into full-time ministry.

You are probably wondering why full-time ministry. In August of the year I graduated high school and was starting at the University of Arizona, my grandfather on my father's side passed away. Days before he died, some of the family were gathered at his bed-side. As we sat conversing, my grandfather looked at one of my aunts and said, "We are going to have a pastor in the family." My aunt laughed and said, "Who are you talking about?" She laughed even more when he pointed at me. My aunt knew my desires in becoming a dentist, so everyone shrugged it off because my grandfather's condition was Alzheimer's. That day, I had zero thoughts about ever becoming a pastor. To add a greater shock factor, when I grad-uated high school just three months prior, I received a gift from one of my other aunts. Receiving a gift for graduation is not shocking, but what the gift was indeed was astonishing. The gift was a leather-bound study Bible with my name engraved on the front. This was the Bible that, while at the University of Arizona, I couldn't put down for some reason. This same Bible was overseas in Naples, Italy, when the chaplain asked me to preach my first sermon, and of course, I preached from this Bible. Yes, in Naples, I would spend three hours a night reading such stories as Jacob and Rachel. Like the Apostle Paul, I'm cur-rently a bivocational pastor, and the words he gave are how I remain working for whom I love.

> Whatever you do, work heartily, as for the Lord and not for men, knowing that from the Lord you will receive the inheri-

tance as your reward. You are serving the
Lord Christ. (Colossians 3:23–24 ESV)

Today my guess is that if your attitude about work is in line with the lyrics below, then you truly understand that the reason for working is because we are working for someone rather than something.

> Take this job and shove it
> I ain't working here no more
> My woman done left and took all the reasons
> I was workin' for
> You better not try to stand in my way
> 'Cause I'm walkin' out the door
> Take this job and shove it
> I ain't workin' here no more.
> (David Allan Coe, "Take This
> Job and Shove It")

We will only discover we have enough when our work is rendered as a service rather than a paycheck.

> For we are His workmanship, created in Christ Jesus for good works, which God prepared beforehand, that we should walk in them. (Ephesians 2:10 ESV)

By understanding this, we truly discover how we find lasting fulfillment in our work, because we are working for the one we love.

Nehemiah is an example of someone working for the one he loved, which was God. Nehemiah left his cushy job as cupbearer in Susa and traveled back to Jerusalem with the sole purpose of rebuilding the turn-down wall around the city. I love the scene where he is up on the wall working and his adversary wants him to come down. He won't come down because he understands he is working for someone greater than this enemy (Nehemiah 6). Knowing he worked for the Lord, Nehemiah did not use his position to take advantages of others but rather honored God in the process by serving them.

> Moreover, from the time that I was appointed to be their governor in the land of Judah, from the twentieth year to the thirty-second year of Artaxerxes the king, twelve years, neither I nor my brothers ate the food allowance of the governor. The former governors who were before me laid heavy burdens on the people and took from them for their daily ration forty shekels of silver. Even their servants lorded it over the people. But I did not do so, because of the fear of God. I also persevered in the work

on this wall, and we acquired no land, and all my servants were gathered there for the work. Moreover, there were at my table 150 men, Jews and officials, besides those who came to us from the nations that were around us. Now what was prepared at my expense for each day was one ox and six choice sheep and birds, and every ten days all kinds of wine in abundance. Yet for all this I did not demand the food allowance of the governor, because the service was too heavy on this people. (Nehemiah 5:14–18 ESV)

When you think about your job, who are you working for? Do you have the same attitude as Nehemiah? When it comes to being satisfied in the job God has given you, are you serving others in the process?

Experiencing Enough

- A big part to loving God is working for the God whom we claim we love.
- In working for God, we put aside selfish desires and allow God to be our fulfillment even if we are in a job we don't like.

- We never find the job God has for us if we don't seek Him.
- Seeking to honor God throughout our career path is how we truly discover fullness.

CHAPTER 4

Winking: A Fatal Attraction

There's a constant contradiction, what
feels good and what feels right.
But, you live with decisions
that you make in your life.
And what steers your direction is hard to understand,
the spirit of a boy, or the wisdom of a man
Now he drives a diesel out of Dallas,
hauling cars out to the coast.
It ain't the dream that he remembered, just a few short years ago.
But tonight at a truckstop,
while drinking a cup,
the waitress grins and winks at him,
and says, "My shift's almost up."
With so much riding on
the choice at hand,

the spirit of a boy, or the wisdom of a man.
With so much riding on
the choice at hand,
the spirit of a boy, or the wisdom of a man.
Trey Bruce and Glen Burtnik, "Spirit
of a Boy, Wisdom of a Man"

My parents just recently celebrated their fortieth wedding anniversary. As I was planning what to say at their party, I decided to look up the popular love songs from the year they got married, which was 1977. Unbeknownst to me, there were several songs about cheating. One such song, since my parents enjoy country music, was the song by Kenny Rogers titled "Lucille." The opening lyric reads, "In a bar in Toledo across from the depot, on a bar stool she took off her ring."

As I ponder what allowed my parents to remain faithful all these years, I remembered how the idea of this book emerged. I was on my way to Sprint car race on a Saturday night. My wife, whom I have been married now to for seven years, was not feeling well. Her condition of rheumatoid arthritis was causing her pain, so she spent the night in bed. Not wanting me to miss out, she said, "Go ahead and go to the races anyways." As I was driving to the track, my mind was pondering the very topic of having enough. In fact, Amy and I the night before had just talked about this idea for a book. I was still in seminary, and my thoughts of God being enough seemed to be in the center as I dealt with school, work, and Amy's condition. I was feeling overwhelmed, so going to the races was a nice treat to wind down. The context of infidelity being linked to the idea of being enough didn't cross my mind until that night, and I am sure glad it did.

Usually, I would meet up with some friends at the races, but for some reason, they all bailed, and I was watching the races solo. About midway through the races, I decided to go get a snack from the snack bar. I wasn't the only one who had the same idea because so did several others. There were probably twelve people ahead of me, and the person directly in front of me was a lady. As we all stood in line, she kept looking back. She didn't look familiar, but not wanting to be rude, I just said hello. She responded back, and we chatted about the races as the line moved forward. As we got near to the front to order, she asked me if I was there alone and proceeded to tell me that she often comes to the races alone. Like that day on the basketball court in chapter 2, I received a prompting. This time, it wasn't a voice but a conviction of knowing exactly what she had in mind. I felt like Joseph when he was allured by Potiphar's wife.

> She caught him by his garment, saying,
> "Lie with me." But he left his garment
> in her hand and fled and got out of the
> house. (Genesis 39:12 ESV)

I, too, quickly fled back to my seat without any other communication. As the races finished, I went directly to my car, and as I was driving home, I thanked God for indeed showing me that the wife he has given me is simply enough.

As I think about whom I should only be winking at, the story of King David comes to mind. King David could do and wink at whomever he wanted because of his power. The problem with using his power as he wished is that David was not only in covenant to his wife but with the God who appointed him as king. David, because he didn't choose to hold on to the idea of God giving him enough, broke rank and went his own way.

> It happened, late one afternoon, when
> David arose from his couch and was walk-
> ing on the roof of the king's house, that
> he saw from the roof a woman bathing;
> and the woman was very beautiful. And
> David sent and inquired about the woman.
> And one said, "Is not this Bathsheba, the
> daughter of Eliam, the wife of Uriah the
> Hittite?" So David sent messengers and

took her, and she came to him, and he
lay with her. (Now she had been purifying
herself from her uncleanness.) Then she
returned to her house. And the woman
conceived, and she sent and told David,
"I am pregnant." (2 Samuel 11:2–5 ESV)

By reading the rest of the chapter, David, in order to cover up his adultery, kills Bathsheba's husband. Of course, nothing is hidden from God, so David is left with the consequences of breaking the oath he had made. I find it fascinating that Scripture says that David is a man after God's own heart. This is said of him before he winks at Bathsheba in 1 Samuel 13:14. Yes, we can and do find ourselves winking and breaking the covenants we have made. The question becomes like David. Do we choose to learn from our mistakes and live as God has actually given us enough? One day, in that study Bible I mentioned in chapter 3, I came across the reason I believe David was given such a title by God. Right before David dies, we discover David, indeed, living at a time when he had nothing to lose, with the mind-set that what God had given him is enough.

Now King David was old and advanced
in years. And although they covered him
with clothes, he could not get warm.
Therefore his servants said to him, "Let a

young woman be sought for my lord the king, and let her wait on the king and be in his service. Let her lie in your arms, that my lord the king may be warm." So they sought for a beautiful young woman throughout all the territory of Israel, and found Abishag the Shunammite, and brought her to the king. The young woman was very beautiful, and she was of service to the king and attended to him, but the king knew her not. (1 Kings 1:1–4 ESV)

King David knew her not, which is the language used in Scripture to denote sexual relations. For example, in the book of Matthew, referring to Joseph, who would take Mary, the mother of Jesus, as his wife, we read, "But knew her not until she had given birth to a son. And he called his name Jesus" (Matthew 1:25 ESV). Also in Genesis, it says the following:

Now Adam knew Eve his wife, and she conceived and bore Cain, saying, "I have gotten a man with the help of the Lord" (Genesis 4:1 ESV)

Cain knew his wife, and she conceived and bore Enoch. (Genesis 4:17 ESV)

Yes, that night at the races, I knew that this lady wanted to "know" me in the way that would violate the covenant I made when I said, "I do." When you look at yourself, have you been winking at things or people you shouldn't? Overcoming this is not corrected by cutting out your eyes but by understanding that God has given you all you need. In case you're wondering what also gave me the strength to say no that night at the races, is because of a personal story in which I, like David, was changed by God.

About eight weeks from my leaving Wichita Falls, I met a girl at what the Navy calls the chow hall. The girl I met was in the Air Force in which they call the common eating place, the dining hall. We struck up a conversation as we waited in line to order our food and then exchanged numbers. She also was at Shepherd Air Force Base, attending school. I would say what her schooling was, but honestly, I don't remember. Neither one of us was married or in any type of dating relationship. I considered myself a Christian, but somehow my mind began to stay focused on her. The very next weekend, we went out, and she came home with me. For some reason, we didn't become "friends with benefits," as today's culture says, on that night, but the next time we saw each other, we fell into that trap. The entire time together, which lasted about four weeks, I was convicted about me "knowing" a female who was not my wife. I believed from God's perspective that sex was and is designed to be practiced in covenant with him in the bonds of marriage. I broke that covenant because I sought out this girl to fill me up instead of allowing God to do that. During this relationship, I was not in fellowship with God—no prayers, no church, no reading the Bible.

Right as this relationship was ending, which I believe because we were only meeting out of lust, I was made aware that I was going to be held back in my schooling for six weeks. I was shocked because I had a 93 percent average in the class. However, my instructors said it was because of my practical skills in being able to make a crown that I needed more practice. The rest of the students in my class were shocked. So much so that they even held a private meeting with the lead instructor. I was told from one of the students that everyone in the class informed the training staff that there was no reason for them to hold me back. By holding me back, there was a possibility I would lose my orders to Italy, in which a week prior I received. This also meant I would spend six weeks more in Texas and not graduate C school with the class I started with. Talk about a hard pill to swallow, which indeed I had to gulp down. My pride, oh my pride, was not happy to say the least. I remember saying, "How dare they hold me back. I have done enough." I surely had done enough, and God was so kindly, reminding me how I had done enough of traveling down the wrong path,

just as he did with David. You see, while I was winking at this girl, I was not longing for the God whom
I said I loved. Being held back, indeed, turned my
focus back to God. Because of God's endless supply
of grace, He turned my shortcoming into a blessing,
allowing me to experience and watch God actually
meet my deepest desires.

I wasn't the only one who was held back; there
was one other student. This student, like me, needed
some extra training, but unlike me, this student was
being used by God. As we waited a week for our new
class to start, we actually got to talk with each other,
and God came up in the conversation. He told me he
was going to church out of town and said I needed
to come for a visit. I did make it to church, and after
church on that first visit, the pastor invited us over for
lunch. I was inspired, not just because the food was
delicious but by their love. I just kept coming back,
attending church often and making friends along the
way. One of those friends happened to be another
person in my new class who also went to the same
church. We would go on our lunch break and pray with
the pastor and a few others who would gather twice
a week to pray at lunchtime. This is what I needed,
a time of being refreshed daily by the God whom I
loved. My time at this church was one of the greatest
experiences I have had, not because I was cured of
my fleshy desire of wanting to be in relationship with a
woman but because God filled that need with Himself.

The pastor had a saying as the single adults gathered on Thursday nights, "You need to date Jesus." This indeed is whom I found myself dating as I finished out my time in Texas. God gives and takes away. What he took from me was what I needed him to take, but what he gave me in return was much greater than my deepest longing. That night at the races, what I was being offered was not worth giving up my marriage or the lasting fulfillment I had found in God—the God who turned me from being held back to giving me more love and joy than I thought was possible.

> All of You is more than enough for all of me
> For every thirst and every need
> You satisfy me with Your love
> And all I have in You is more than enough
>
> You are my supply
> My breath of life
> And still more awesome than I know
> You are my reward
> worth living for
> And still more awesome than I know
>
> All of You is more than enough for all of me
> For every thirst and every need
> You satisfy me with Your love
> And all I have in You is more than enough.
> (Chris Tomlin, "Enough")

Experiencing Enough

- By allowing the words from Chris Tomlin's song to become our anthem, we discover especially in the context of our marriages the type of intimacy that is both satisfying and lasting.
- We will never allow our marriage to be enough if we are seeking pleasure from someone else.
- This is also true in our relationship with God, which is why we are called to love Him with our entire being.
- We cannot keep our eyes focused on the covenant God has with us when are winking at anything or anybody else.

CHAPTER 5

Wronging: People Are Your Customer

I didn't cheat, I didn't lie
So her leaving took me by surprise
Just a note on the table say-
ing we're though
At first I went crazy, so it
took me some time
But I finally read between the lines
It's not what I did
It's what I didn't do.
Wood Newton and Michael
Noble, "What I Didn't Do"

Up above the door of the barbershop I used to frequent is a sign that reads, "I would rather have one customer a hundred times than 100 customers one time." The reality of this sign being true takes effort. I would love to say that in my past relationships I have always had concern for others and a desire of always wanting to keep them around. However, as I look at my life now through the lens of being wronged, I can say I am not ashamed when I read such passages as shared below. The reason for this is because of a few life lessons and a continual reading through these words from the Apostle James on multiple occasions.

> What causes quarrels and what causes fights among you? Is it not this, that your passions are at war within you? You desire and do not have, so you murder. You covet and cannot obtain, so you fight and quarrel. You do not have, because you do not ask. You ask and do not receive, because you ask wrongly, to spend it on your passions. You adulterous people! Do you not know that friendship with the world is enmity with God? Therefore whoever wishes to be a friend of the world makes himself an enemy of God. Or do you suppose it is to no purpose that the Scripture says, "He yearns jealously over the spirit that he has made to dwell in us"? But he gives more grace. Therefore it says, "God opposes the proud but gives grace to the humble." Submit yourselves therefore to God. Resist the devil, and he will flee from you. Draw near to God, and he will

draw near to you. Cleanse your hands, you sinners, and purify your hearts, you double-minded. Be wretched and mourn and weep. Let your laughter be turned to mourning and your joy to gloom. Humble yourselves before the Lord, and he will exalt you. Do not speak evil against one another, brothers. The one who speaks against a brother or judges his brother, speaks evil against the law and judges the law. But if you judge the law, you are not a doer of the law but a judge. There is only one lawgiver and judge, he who is able to save and to destroy. But who are you to judge your neighbor? (James 4:1–12 ESV)

I didn't always respond in humility, like I do today, which was proven when I got kicked out of a coffee shop. This was only a few years after I left the Navy, and unfortunately, I lived with the notion "The customer is always right." I would go to this coffee shop daily, and quite often, I found myself asking them to remake my coffee. My request was not huge; I simply wanted my latte with no foam. To my frustration, the barista couldn't seem to make my latte free of foam. I didn't feel that I was rude but would ask nicely for them to remake the drink. The franchise owner happened to see this on a few occasions and had enough with me asking them to remake the drink. His response to me was, "What you do to these girls is disgraceful, and you are not welcomed here any longer." For some reason, I was able to keep my cool, and I never went back.

Initially, my thought was to call and complain and say how I have been wronged. As a day or two passed, I remembered I would sit at this coffee shop and read my Bible and other religious books. One of the books I remember reading there is a book titled *They Smell like Sheep* by Lynn Anderson. The premise of the book is how shepherds should smell like their flock and how shepherds should lay down their life for their sheep. As I thought about this book, I realized in a roundabout way this coffee shop owner was a sheep who needed to be shepherded. Whether I liked it or not, I needed to at least treat him as the Good Shepherd has treated me. I didn't end up calling but used this story to be my reminder of what it looks like to work through being wronged.

> The very fact that you have lawsuits among you means you have been completely defeated already. Why not rather be wronged? Why not rather be cheated? Instead, you yourselves cheat and do wrong, and you do this to your brothers and sisters. (1 Corinthians 6:7–8 NIV)

Fast forward a few years, and I was given the opportunity to supervise at a particular post office in Phoenix. I was asked to leave the station I had been working at to be the opening supervisor at a different station. This station was one that had difficulty in performing and meeting standards. After working there for a few months, I discovered an issue that happened to be an employee. From my observation, this particular employee would not only call in sick quite often but would refuse to work at the level of the rest of the employees. This led to multiply conversations about her performance, and nothing changed. I talked to my boss about it, and she also had words with the employee. According to the employee, we were picking on her, so she filed an official complaint, which required mediation. I had never been to mediation, so I didn't know what to expect.

As we get to the mediation, it's my boss and her boss, along with the employee, a union representative for the employee, me, and a third-party mediator. The mediator's job was to help both sides come to a resolution. For some reason, about halfway through, a break was given in which my boss's boss told me that I could let loose and tell the employee how much of a piece of crap she was or use any other language I wanted to against this employee. Not really knowing what to say, I just said okay, and we proceeded back into the mediation. My turn came to speak, and I didn't speak as the boss suggested but simply how I just needed the employee to work like the rest of the employees. The mediation ended, and we all got up to leave the meeting, which was actually at our station. The mediator happened to walk to the side exit, which needed to be locked behind her for security purposes, so I followed her to the door. I never met this woman before, but she turned to me and said, "I just want to thank you for how you handled yourself in the mediation." She gave me a smile as if I made her day and said, "God bless you." For me, this was a reminder that how we treat others is important. Yes, how we handle others who have wronged us is crucial. Why? Because the world is always watching.

> Love is patient, love is kind. It does not envy, it does not boast, it is not proud. It does not dishonor others, it is not self-seeking, it is not easily angered, it keeps no record of wrongs. Love does not delight in evil but rejoices with the truth. It always protects, always trusts, always hopes, always perseveres. (1 Corinthians 13:4–7 NIV)

How do you respond when you are wronged? Is it out of love or out or hate? My encouragement to you as I have learned is to lean toward grace and away from proving how right you are.

> Good sense makes one slow to anger,
> and it is his glory to overlook an offense.
> (Proverbs 19:11 ESV)

In a cultural where no one likes admitting they are wrong but everyone wants justice for being wronged, we must take a different approach. The kind of approach like the Apostle Peter witnessed firsthand as we walked with Christ.

> For to this you have been called, because Christ also suffered for you, leaving you an example, so that you might follow in his steps. He committed no sin, neither was deceit found in his mouth. When he was reviled, he did not revile in return; when he suffered, he did not threaten, but continued entrusting himself to him who judges justly. He himself bore our sins in his body on the tree, that we might die to sin and live to righteousness. By his wounds you have been healed. (1 Peter 2:21–24 ESV)

The reason for not embracing this Christ-like attitude is because by not getting even, we assume we are missing out on teaching the other person a lesson. However, in realty, what we are telling God in this situation is that God hasn't done enough so we need to respond. We need to say or do something to fulfill our need for more. Yes, more justice, more punishment, more showing how right I am. By understanding when it comes to being wronged that God is enough and respond accordingly, we uncover how God's love is indeed enough to right the wrong.

You might be wondering why I chose the song lyric I did to start this chapter. Better yet, wouldn't these lyrics fit better with the last chapter? Actually the words to this song and the lyrics I conclude with, speak to both topics. Why, because when it comes to being wronged, often the relationships we experience being slighted the most in, is our marriages. This is why I picked the songs I did for this chapter and bring them into this conversion regarding being wronged. Every marriage relationship I have observed, including my own, all fail and succeed by how each individual in the relationship handles being wronged. What we do and don't do when one is feeling that they have been mistreated is crucial. As the expression proclaims, "a little grace goes a long way." Grace is important within any relationship, but it is extremely valuable when interacting with your spouse. When it comes to your marriage or dating relationship, are you graceful when you have been offended by the person whom you love? Jesus, as he spoke on the mountain, had this to say about being ill-treated. "You have heard that it was said, 'An eye for an eye and a tooth for a tooth.' But I say to you, do not resist the one who is evil. But if anyone slaps you on the right cheek, turn to him the other also." (Matthew 5:38-39 ESV)

Yes, I agree, Jesus is talking about our enemies wronging us, which proves even more so how we should respond out of grace to those who we have a loving relationship with.

My guess is, as I have learned, you also would agree, that when we have wronged our spouses or feel wronged by them, giving and receiving grace always builds a bridge, instead of installing a fence between each other. Consequently, even what I don't say matters, which is why, what is not said or done should be considered a wronging as well. Yes, grace is how we overcome being wronged and no marriage or dating relationship stands the test of time without overcoming each other's wrongs.

> I would whisper love so loudly, every heart could understand
> Love and only love can join the tribes of man
> I would give my heart's desire so that you might see
> The first step is to realize that it all begins with you and me. Love can build a bridge
> Between your heart and mine
> Love can build a bridge
> Don't you think it's time?
> Don't you think it's time? (John Barlow et al., "Love Can Build a Bridge")

Experiencing Enough

- We will never fill our bank of love if we keep dishing out hate or releasing the dam of revenge.
- Getting even doesn't allow room for God's grace and love to abound.
- Next time your food order or latte is made wrong, accept it anyways and watch God grant you peace.
- Remember, turning the other cheek is not a lesson for the one turning but to the one who is doing the striking.

CHAPTER 6

Wasting: Another Leads to Another

> She put him out like the burnin'
> end of a midnight cigarette
> She broke his heart he spent
> his whole life tryin' to forget
> We watched him drink his pain
> away a little at a time
> But he never could get drunk
> enough to get her off his mind
> Until the night.
> Jon Randall and Bill Anderson,
> "Whiskey Lullaby"

I remember that night well; it was a Saturday night, and the clock showed eleven thirty. My wife and I were in bed, and my cell phone rang. It was my best friend, whom I have known since kindergarten. From the tone in his voice, I could tell not all was well. He wanted to know what would happen to him spiritually if he ended it that night. From what I gathered from our conversation, he had been drinking since Thursday, and the alcohol was in full destruction mode. Not sure exactly what to say, I just kept reassuring him that this wasn't the end because he wasn't going to go out in this way. My wife, who happens to be very familiar with what being controlled by alcohol looks like, said, "We must go get him." Somehow, after about twenty minutes, I was able to convince my friend that not only was I going to pick him up but that he was staying with us for the remaining of the weekend. Not knowing what to expect, I made the hour drive in one direction to pick him up. Upon arrival, he was alone in his roommate's house, pacing back and forth. The large bottle of vodka was nearing empty, and he was emotional. We made the hour trek back, talked a bit when we got home, and then went to bed.

As the day dawned and we all arose, my friend actually got up and went to church with us. Going to church each week was our normal Sunday routine. After church, we always gathered for lunch with our small group, and he also came to that. He didn't talk, but he witnessed those in the group welcome him as if he had been there every week. By the end of the weekend, he was clear-minded enough to accept our plea to stay with us. He took us up on the offer and ended up staying with us for two months before he enrolled into the Salvation Army Drug and Rehabilitation Program. I know what you are thinking. Are you crazy? You let someone who was suicidal and under the influence stay with you. This is where the story gets good.

Six months prior to this, my friend had an accident as he was driving to an out-of-town wedding with his daughter. Not a shocker, but he was driving under the influence on an already expended license for a previous DUI. To put you at ease, his daughter made it through the accident without any injuries, but my friend was taken to the hospital. During his couple days' stay in the hospital, we had heard about the accident and drove the two-and-a-half-hour drive north to see him in the hospital. We did the friendly thing. We visited for a while and then headed home. On the way home, my wife and I talked about my friend and him needing help. For some reason, the topic of him moving in with us was brought up, and we both agreed right there on that day that we would allow him to move in with us if the opportunity arose. I never told my friend this, so that night when we got the call, we felt the decision was already made for us. Fast forward almost five years, through loosing custody of his daughter, finishing the six-month rehab program, meeting his wonderful soon-to-be wife, spending four months in prison, having a son, and regaining split custody with his daughter, my friend has remained clean and sober since that night.

I am not sure why God chose us to walk this journey with my friend, but I do know it was life or death. In these types of situations, sometimes you need the help of others. This reminds me of when I was about five years of age. My dad used to drink beer by the gallon from what I was told. So much so that if he didn't finish the beer he was drinking the night before, my mom would put a plastic cap over the can for my dad to drink the next day. I was old enough that I could go get my dad a beer when he asked me to. I started, for whatever reason, opening new cans and drinking some out then placing one of those plastic caps on it and then taking it to my dad. My mom caught me doing this and told my dad, but he didn't believe her. My dad told my mom, after she caught me doing it again for the umpteenth time, that if he caught me doing what my mom was saying I was doing, then he would quit drinking altogether. Well, lo and behold, one night my dad decided to watch me closely and I was caught in the act. "Thanks to my mom's persistence and God's leading" my dad that night owned up to the promise he made my mom and dumped out his beer and stopped drinking completely. As I ponder this story and the story of my friend, another story comes to mind. Yes, the continual story of God honoring the promise to bless his children instead of allowing them to waste away.

The children of Israel had found themselves in slavery because of their own actions of not listening to God (Genesis 26 and 50). They spend many years in slavery in Egypt and cried out to God to rescue them. This story is called the Exodus because God moves heaven and earth so they could both exit the hands of Pharaoh and Egypt. What they needed to be was delivered, and God indeed delivered them in a mighty way.

> Then the LORD said to Moses, "Stretch out your hand over the sea, that the water may come back upon the Egyptians, upon their chariots, and upon their horsemen." So Moses stretched out his hand over the sea, and the sea returned to its normal course when the morning appeared. And as the Egyptians fled into it, the LORD threw the Egyptians into the midst of the sea. The waters returned and covered the chariots and the horsemen; of all the host of Pharaoh that had followed them into the sea, not one of them remained. But the people of Israel walked on dry ground through the sea, the waters being a wall to them on their right hand and on their left. Thus the LORD saved Israel that day from the hand of the Egyptians, and Israel saw the Egyptians dead on the seashore. Israel saw the great power

that the LORD used against the Egyptians,
so the people feared the LORD, and they
believed in the LORD and in his servant
Moses. (Exodus 14:26–31 ESV)

One doesn't have to be under the influence to
need deliverance. All of us face things in our life in
which we needed to be delivered from. What allows
one to be delivered is by understanding that God is
able. In simple terms, we must know that God has
enough capacity to do so. If you were to ask my dad,
my friend, and those who made it into the Promised
Land if God was enough to deliver them, they all
would say yes. They say yes because like the disci-
ples who witnessed Jesus being raised from the dead
and later the Apostle Paul, there was no question if
they had enough to overcome any obstacle.

What then shall we say to these things?
If God is for us, who can be against
us? He who did not spare his own Son
but gave him up for us all, how will he
not also with him graciously give us
all things? Who shall bring any charge
against God's elect? It is God who justi-
fies. Who is to condemn? Christ Jesus is
the one who died—more than that, who

was raised—who is at the right hand of God, who indeed is interceding for us. (Romans 8:31–34 ESV)

I had the privilege of walking with my friend through rehab and him experiencing how God proved to him that he was more than enough to deliver him from wasting away. On several occasions, I spent time watching my friend and his fellow beneficiaries at the Salvation Army's chapel service. The song they loved to sing didn't make sense to me as to why they would choose to sing it, especially since they all were in the same situation—treading water, hoping to be rescued before they drowned. However, thinking about it through the lens that God is enough, I know now why they sang it at the top of their lungs.

Are you wasting away, or are you allowing God to deliver you? God, as with Israel, my friend, along with conquering sin and death through Christ, is more than enough to rescue you from being enslaved by any addiction. When individuals embrace this truth, they truly discover that life is not worth wasting but celebrating. There is no better way to rejoice than to join the countless others in singing the same song as they marched to being delivered.

I was sure by now

God You would have reached down
And wiped our tears away
Stepped in and saved the day
But once again, I say "Amen," and it's
still raining

As the thunder rolls
I barely hear Your whisper through the rain
"I'm with you"
And as Your mercy falls
I raise my hands and praise the God who
gives
And takes away

(Chorus)
And I'll praise You in this storm
And I will lift my hands
For You are who You are
No matter where I am
And every tear I've cried
You hold in Your hand
You never left my side
And though my heart is torn
I will praise You in this storm

I remember when
I stumbled in the wind
You heard my cry to you
And you raised me up again

My strength is almost gone
How can I carry on
If I can't find You

But as the thunder rolls
I barely hear You whisper through the rain
"I'm with you"
And as Your mercy falls
I raise my hands and praise the God who
gives
And takes away

(Chorus)
I lift my eyes unto the hills
Where does my help come from?
My help comes from the Lord
The Maker of Heaven and Earth
(Mark Hall and Bernie Herms,
"Praise You in This Storm")

Experiencing Enough

- By wasting our time on temporary things, we miss out on experiencing that which is permanent.
- Addictions only enslave individuals to keep using while God frees us up to enjoy more and more of Him.

- Our help has arrived; the question is, are you allowing God, who is the help, to remove your dependencies?
- Jesus died to save lives from being wasted and how you avoid wasting yours is by embracing Him.

CHAPTER 7

Welcoming: Rendering a Salute

Don't give up
Because you want to burn bright
If darkness blinds you
I, I will shine to guide you
Everybody wants to be understood
Well I can hear you
Everybody wants to be loved
Don't give up
Because you are loved, you are loved.
Thomas Salter, "You Are Loved"

One of the greatest feelings for me during my five years of naval service was coming home. The welcome you receive and being able to enjoy that favorite food spot, hanging out with family, or going to a sporting event made the long trip home worthwhile. During my last year of active duty, I was able to come home for two weeks during Christmas. I was stationed in Pensacola, Florida, so I had to fly to Atlanta, Georgia, and then fly from Atlanta to Phoenix. To save money, I booked in early flight, which put me in Atlanta at seven in the morning. I exited the plane and then headed to find my gate. I believe my layover in Atlanta was about an hour and a half. I found my gate, and my flight was on time, so I headed to find me something to eat. Not too far from the gate was a place that was serving breakfast sandwiches and my favorite beverage coffee. A few others had the same idea, and there was a line.

While standing in line, a soldier passed by in desert camouflage and had a backpack draped over his shoulder. He appeared to be heading down to a different gate. As I moved up to the front of the line, I felt compelled to go find this soldier and thank him for his service. I convinced myself that I needed to stay in line and then do something about how I felt after I ordered. You know the game we play with ourselves. We are convicted about something but tell ourselves some excuse. Well, this was me that day. I ordered and then went back to my gate. As I started to eat my sandwich, the conviction got stronger, so I ate quickly and proceeded to find this stranger. I walked down to the other gates and couldn't find this soldier. At the end of the gate, there actually was a USO room, where they had a place for military members to hang out at. I looked into the room, but there were no soldiers in camouflage. There was a table with refreshments and volunteers who, from what I can recall, were giving out cookies and drinks. Honestly, I didn't know, when I found this soldier, what I was going to tell him. I just had this deep feeling that he was just coming back from being deployed and he needed to know someone cared for him. I don't think he was a ghost or angel, but what happened after this might seem paranormal.

I made it home that afternoon and had a wonderful welcoming. That night, as we often did, my parents and I prayed together before we went to bed. We all took turns praying, and as I started praying, once again I was concerned about this soldier and even shed some tears. I not only prayed for him but for our military. At this time, the hunt to track down the leaders responsible for 9/11 was in full force. I prayed that our military would succeed and be protected in the process. We ended the nightly prayer and went to bed. As we woke up the next morning, which happened to be my mother's birthday, December 13, the news story that was being talked about on every channel was the capture of Saddam Hussein. Yes, I agree there is no direct connection to what took place at the airport to the capture of Saddam Hussein. However, there is a broader lesson that reminds me of how God longs to give us a warm welcoming home all because he cares. That soldier, that prayer, that news within the same context simply allowed me to see once again God showing his great love—the same love and care we see ever present in the story known as "The Prodigal Son."

Jesus continued: "There was a man who had two sons. The younger one said to his father, 'Father, give me my share of the estate.' So he divided his property between them. Not long after that, the younger son got together all he had, set off for a distant country and there squandered his wealth in wild living. After he had spent everything, there was a severe famine in that whole country, and he began to be in need. So he went and hired himself out to a citizen of that country, who sent him to his fields to feed pigs. He longed to fill his stomach with the pods that the pigs were eating, but no one gave him anything. When he came to his senses, he said, 'How many of my father's hired servants have food to spare, and here I am starving to death! I will set out and go back to my father and say to him: "Father, I have sinned against heaven and against you. I am no longer worthy to be called your son; make me like one of your hired servants."' So he got up and went to his father. But while he was still a long way off, his father saw him and was filled with compassion for him; he ran to his son, threw his arms around him and kissed him. The son said to him, 'Father, I have sinned against heaven and against you. I am no longer worthy to be called your son.' But the father said to his servants, 'Quick! Bring the best robe and put it on him. Put a ring on his finger and sandals on his feet. Bring the fattened calf and kill it. Let's have a feast and celebrate. For this son of mine was dead and is alive again; he was lost and is found.' So they began to celebrate." (Luke 15:11–24 NIV)

This story of the lost son helps me understand why I was not only given the story at the airport but two other stories that have solidified for me that God has and is working behind the scenes. The reason for him working on my behalf is to show me that, indeed, He is enough. By Him welcoming me, I see firsthand that He is not only capable but is able to fill my every emotional, spiritual, and physical need.

The year was 1996, and we just arrived back from an unsuccessful hunting trip in Southern Arizona. My dad and I were dropping off my dad's little brother at his house in Tucson so we could head back to our house in Phoenix. When we arrived at his house, there was a note on his door asking us to contact one of the girls, which meant their sisters. Of course, we called and discovered that one of their brothers passed away the night before in his sleep. The news was devastating, to say the least, but there was nothing we could do to help at the moment, so we headed back to Phoenix. The drive from Tucson to Phoenix takes two hours, and we were about thirty minutes into the drive. My dad, who was close to his brother, was emotional, and it was actually only one of the few times I have seen my dad cry. My dad said we needed to pray, so we started to pray as we drove home. My dad prayed for the family and especially his brother's family, including his kids and wife, whom he left behind. We had just finished praying, and on the side of the road in which we were approaching was a green road sign displaying the mileage for some of the upcoming cities. On the bottom left corner of the sign, in the blank green area, was another sign that was smaller and white in color with black letters. The letters made up two words: "Trust Jesus." Both my father and I, even though we were Christians, understood the sign due to the circumstances to mean much more. We never saw the sign again even though we kept looking for it on many trips back to Phoenix from Tucson. This sign showed me then and reminds me today, along with all the other stories I have lived through, that I am loved—not simply loved to get something in return but loved with arms wide open, as if God is welcoming home and is saying, "Let's celebrate!"

The second story is found in the pages of Scripture and is known as the book of Ruth. In this four-chapter book, we find another story about God's children not lacking even despite tragedy. Chapter 1 opens with a famine in the land, so Naomi and her husband, with their two boys in tow, move to Moab. They get to Moab, and their boys, as they grow older, find wives, and each of them gets married. Disaster strikes, and not only does Nomi loose her husband, but as time goes on, she also loses her two boys. Not wanting to be a hindrance to her daughters-in-law, Naomi decides to move back to her home town, Bethlehem. A debate arises among Naomi and the daughters-in-law about not wanting to leave Naomi. Naomi doesn't want them to come, but she is only able to convince one to stay. Ruth, on the other hand, refuses to stay and travels back with Naomi to Bethlehem. At the end of the chapter, they arrive in Bethlehem during the barley harvest.

Chapter 2 to 4 all deal with both Ruth and Naomi being provided and cared for. Yes, all their needs are going to be met all because of a character named Boaz. Boaz is going to save the day by him redeeming Ruth from her tragedy.

> Then Boaz announced to the elders and all the people, "Today you are witnesses that I have bought from Naomi all the property of Elimelek, Kilion and

Mahlon. I have also acquired Ruth the Moabite, Mahlon's widow, as my wife, in order to maintain the name of the dead with his property, so that his name will not disappear from among his family or from his hometown. Today you are witnesses!" Then the elders and all the people at the gate said, "We are witnesses. May the Lord make the woman who is coming into your home like Rachel and Leah, who together built up the family of Israel. May you have standing in Ephrathah and be famous in Bethlehem. Through the offspring the Lord gives you by this young woman, may your family be like that of Perez, whom Tamar bore to Judah." So Boaz took Ruth and she became his wife. When he made love to her, the Lord enabled her to conceive, and she gave birth to a son. The women said to Naomi: "Praise be to the Lord, who this day has not left you without a guardian-redeemer. May he become famous throughout Israel! He will renew your life and sustain you in your old age. For your daughter-in-law, who loves you and who is better to you than seven sons, has given him birth." Then Naomi took the child in her arms and cared for him. The women living there said, "Naomi has a son!" And they named him Obed. He was the father of Jesse, the father of David. (Ruth 4:9–16 NIV)

Boaz welcomed Ruth with the same kind of love and care that God showed Boaz's family in the past. In case you didn't know, Boaz is the son of Rehab, the ex-prostitute whom God spared when the walls of Jericho fell (Joshua 6). By God welcoming Rehab, her son was able to show the same kind of care and concern to Ruth. It's these stories that in the course of my life God has over and over again proven himself to be enough. Because I am not found lacking, I am full of praise and thanksgiving to God alone, who indeed has rescued me from the false notion that I need more. I don't need more because the God of the universe continues to welcome me with an abundance of ongoing love and grace. Have you discovered this kind of welcoming? If you haven't, I am confident, like the Prodigal Son, God is waiting for you with open arms. Not only to rescue you from the lie of needing more but to completely satisfy your eternal soul.

Just as I am, Thou wilt receive,
Wilt welcome, pardon, cleanse, relieve;
Because Thy promise I believe,
O Lamb of God, I come, I come.

Just as I am, Thy love unknown
Hath broken every barrier down;
Now, to be Thine, yea, Thine alone,
O Lamb of God, I come, I come.
Just as I am, of that free love
The breadth, length, depth,
and height to prove,
Here for a season, then above,
O Lamb of God, I come, I come!
Charlotte Elliot, "Just As I Am"

Experiencing Enough

- God's homecoming is always greater than you feel you deserve.
- Today is always a good day to travel home to God.
- Once you're home, your action is simply to invite others to the party as well.
- God's welcoming party is always ongoing, and His resources never run out.

CONCLUSION

A Beginning to the End

As you now have finished these stories, both of mine and from pages of old, I hope you don't leave with these two concluding thoughts. The first is the notion that I am some type of superhuman. I, like you, am an ordinary person with a run-of-the-mill kind of job and am part of conventional family. I am just as James says about Elijah the Prophet:

> Elijah was a man with a nature like ours, and he prayed fervently that it might not rain, and for three years and six months it did not rain on the earth. Then he prayed again, and heaven gave rain, and the earth bore its fruit. (James 5:17–18)

Like Elijah, I have seen and experienced some not-so-ordinary things. Yes, like the time the car broke because it just stalled as we were driving. My dad was able to steer the car and bring it to a stop on the side of the road. He began turning it over and over again, but it wouldn't start. Before he popped the hood, he said, "Let's pray." My dad prayed, and then to our surprise, as he turned it over one more time, before getting out to raise the hood, the car started.

I, like every other person, struggle with stepping onto the hamster wheel of more. Whether it is in wanting the latest and greatest to lusting as I spot a beautiful girl or dreaming what my life would be like if I won the lottery, I am no different. Yes, in moments like these, I am reminded of my humanness. My fleshly desires want to get the best of me. However, what I have learned is that, through recalling these stories, I discover the antidote, which is turning to the one who is enough. This is exactly what Daniel's three friends did when they refused to bow down to King Nebuchadnezzar's golden image.

> Shadrach, Meshach, and Abednego answered and said to the king, "O Nebuchadnezzar, we have no need to answer you in this matter. If this be so, our God whom we serve is able to deliver us from the burning fiery furnace, and he will deliver us out of your hand, O king. But if not, be it known to you, O king, that we will not serve your gods or wor-

ship the golden image that you have set
up." (Daniel 3:16–18 ESV)

When we live and let God be our portion, no matter what we face or long for, we step off the rat race of needing more and dive into the ever-expanding pool of abundant life.

The second thought, I hope you are not holding onto as we part ways, is the idea that these Bible stories have no meaning for you. It's easy to find yourself saying what happened with these individuals happened with them but will never happen to me. I bet, like me, as you look back on your own life there is a story or two where God was not only trying to get your attention but was longing for you to turn to Him for satisfaction. Yes, the story you recall could, like King Belshazzar, be tragic. "This is the interpretation of the matter: Mene, God has numbered the days of your kingdom and brought it to an end; Tekel, you have been weighed in the balances and found wanting; Peres, your kingdom is divided and given to the Medes and Persians" (Daniel 5:26–28 ESV). But unlike this king, you are still here. Yes, God is not through with you yet. I don't normally promise people anything, but I am confident that when we trust in God in any area of life, like Daniel and countless others has done throughout history, we will not be found wanting like King Belshazzar. The question becomes, are you allowing God to prove this in you? If you are, please share your stories with others. Why? Because others need to know what you have discovered. If not, I plead with you to be like Gideon (Judges 6:36–40) that in any of the seven areas of your life—wanting, winning, working, winking, wronging, wasting, or welcoming—you throw out a fleece and allow God to prove who He is. What you will discover is not that you need more but that He is the one who is actually able to quench your thirst of wanting more. May you indeed find the one who is and will always be enough.

> Some wandered in desert wastes, finding no way to a city to dwell in; hungry and thirsty, their soul fainted within them. Then they cried to the LORD in their trouble, and he delivered them from their distress. He led them by a straight way till they reached a city to dwell in. Let them thank the LORD for his steadfast love, for his wondrous works to the children of man! For he satisfies the longing soul, and the hungry soul he fills with good things. (Psalm 107:4–9 ESV)

EPILOGUE

Beyond the memory

In 2010, my dad and I decided to take a drive to look for a new hunting spot. My dad wanted to check out an area that was not too many miles from where his parents used to own a home and forty acres. We traveled where my dad wanted to scout and then decided, because we had some time left, to take a trip by the old homestead. This is the place that the younger children were raised and my grandfather ranched and hunted and lived off the land. From the main highway, you are required to travel up a few mile-long unpaved road, cross a wash, and go up a pretty steep hill to get to the old house. Right before you get up the hill, my grandfather had two wood poles and a chain that could be strung across so people couldn't drive up to the house. As we approached this area of the road on that day, the chain was strung across. The property no longer belonged to our family because after my grandmother passed, a few years prior the property and house was sold to a family member of the neighbor who lived down the road about three quarters of a mile. We decided to get out and look around before we backed down the hill. We had just crawled out of our vehicle when a truck came barreling up the road. A man jumped out and said, "What are you guys doing up here?" We nicely said who we were, and he recognized our last name. We proceeded to tell him that we just wanted to see if anything had changed on the old house and property. Knowing who we were by him being my grandfather's neighbor for many years, he changed his initial response of us being possible intruders to striking up a conversation.

At this time, my grandfather had been deceased almost twelve years, but this neighbor insisted on telling us how much my grandfather had an impact on him over the years. He began to tell us a story about a time in the early 1980s when a huge storm hit their valley and Tucson, trapping them in their homes. The wash you have to cross to get to both of their properties was completed flooded. The water level in the wash was approximately nine to ten feet deep and many feet wide. To the neighbor's nightmare, one of their children, a baby at that time, was extremely sick and had a very high fever. They called my grandparents, asking my grandfather how possible it would to be for them to ride on their horses to town with their baby so that their precious child could get the needed help. The neighbor even called the National Guard to fly them out, but they were so busy in town with rescuing all the cars stuck in washes that they couldn't give him a time frame as to when they could rescue "the child" from their mountain home. They didn't know what to do, but about eight o'clock that night, my grandfather rode over to the neighbor's house on his horse. My grandfather told the neighbor, "I don't know what else to do for you. All I know to do is to simply pray for you and your child." My grandfather prayed and went home. By morning of the next day, the neighbor discovered that the fever had broken. After the fever went down, the child was on the road to recovery.

Standing on the hill that day and hearing this story wasn't shocking because of my grandfather's faith. However, this was the first time our family had ever heard that story. As I look back to this story given on the hill that day, I know what my grandfather was doing before he finally headed over to their house that night. Yes, praying, but wondering what he should do. Like me, I bet he was debating if he should act or not, should ride over or not. I can imagine seeing him doing what I did that day as I stood in line as the soldier passed me at the Atlanta Airport. Needless to say, my grandfather did go over, and years later, it is why I decided to share with you this closing story and what has followed after.

You see, about four months after we chatted with my grandfather's old neighbor, the neighbor was killed, actually murdered on what appeared to be business deal gone wrong. I find myself today wondering what would have happened if I shared with him what God had been showing me. What if I would have shared with this neighbor that the reason he had that story is because God was showing him how to discover enough? Yes, revealing to this neighbor that the reason my grandfather did go over and pray was not simply because my grandfather was a good man, although he was, but because of God using my grandfather to remind the neighbor that even despite natural disasters and sickness God cares and meets your every need. Who knows, maybe that day I could have changed the course of that neighbor's life as God has done with mine. I honestly don't know the relationship this neighbor had with the Lord. What I do know is that this story God had given him back in the 1980s was to show him how God meets us in our greatest longings.

This leads us to today, where we are able to see the whole picture. The picture of how God uses both the stories of our life and the stories of others, both personal and from Scripture, to show us why we need to embrace Him alone. On May 8, 2017, the Mulberry Fire swept through the valley of the ole homestead. To honor those who lost their home, I will not share with you who lost their home but will share with you one of the homes that didn't burn. We got word about a week later that it burned all around my grandparents' old house but didn't touch the house, although I feel for those neighbors who lost their houses, and many years of memories, this Scripture comes to mind.

> Everyone then who hears these words of mine and does them will be like a wise man who built his house on the rock. And the rain fell, and the floods came, and the winds blew and beat on that house, but it did not fall, because it had been founded on the rock. And everyone who hears these words of mine and does not do them will be like a foolish man who built his house on the sand. And the rain fell, and the floods came, and the winds blew and beat against that house, and it fell, and great was the fall of it. (Matthew 7:24–27 ESV)

You might be thinking, how do these words bring comfort to someone who has lost so much? This is the reason for writing this book. I cannot—my efforts fall short—but God can. He is able to quench our deepest longing and need. The reason for giving this verse is because I was there that day when the foundation was laid on my grandparents' old house.

This family building project was an all-hands-on-deck eleven-day ordeal. My grandparents only had a house trailer for a dwelling. The family decided to build an addition on the front of the trailer. The renovation would give my grandparents a new living room, bathroom, and a kitchen with a nice covered porch and a swing. My grandparents were sent on a vacation to Oklahoma, and during their vacation, we toiled, and they came home to a new surprise, an addition that love built.

I say *love* because God showed his love to us as we were building. An old station wagon that was parked out front of the trailer needed to be moved. The solution was to use a boom forklift to drag and pull the car down the hill, parking it off to the side. The car and forklift were connected by a chain. The process of moving the car went well until the chain broke. As the saying goes, "What goes up must come down," and down the hill the car went. This wouldn't have been a big deal, but everyone else's cars were parked at the bottom of the hill. For some strange reason, the car hit a bump, maybe because all the tires were flat, and made a hard turn. The car turned, rolled over the berm, and literally stopped in the place where we were going to park the car in the first place.

After my grandparents both passed and the family sold the house, the new owners removed the old trailer and left the addition as we had built it. Other than pouring a concrete slab behind where the trailer was, the house remained the same. As I looked at the pictures of what the fire burnt, you can tell the fire surrounded the home but the house didn't fall because the flames never reached the house. Could it be that once again God is making himself known? Yes, God is proclaiming for the watching world to see that we need to build our lives on Him. God again, through this present story, is showing us that despite what we face, like this widowed neighbor, God is enough. He is enough now and will always be enough to keep our lives standing even in the midst of the fire. The question is, are you and will you allow God to be who He is and that is *enough*?

> And the satraps, the prefects, the governors, and the king's counselors gathered together and saw that the fire had not had any power over the bodies of those men. The hair of their heads was not singed, their cloaks were not harmed, and no smell of fire had come upon them. Nebuchadnezzar answered and said, "Blessed be the God of Shadrach, Meshach, and Abednego, who has sent his angel and delivered his servants, who trusted in him, and set aside the king's command, and yielded up their bodies rather than serve and worship any god except their own God." (Daniel 3:27–28 ESV)

ABOUT THE AUTHOR

Mike Hoffman is a pastor and a Navy veteran who holds a bachelor's degree from Grand Canyon University and master of ministry in leadership development from Phoenix Seminary. As a shepherd and leader, Mike has led and helped hundreds of individuals over the past decade discover how God meets our deepest longings.

CPSIA information can be obtained
at www.ICGtesting.com
Printed in the USA
BVHW04s1356140518
516179BV00002B/251/P